Spiders Everywh[ere]

by Betty L. Baker

illustrated by Judith Pfeiffer

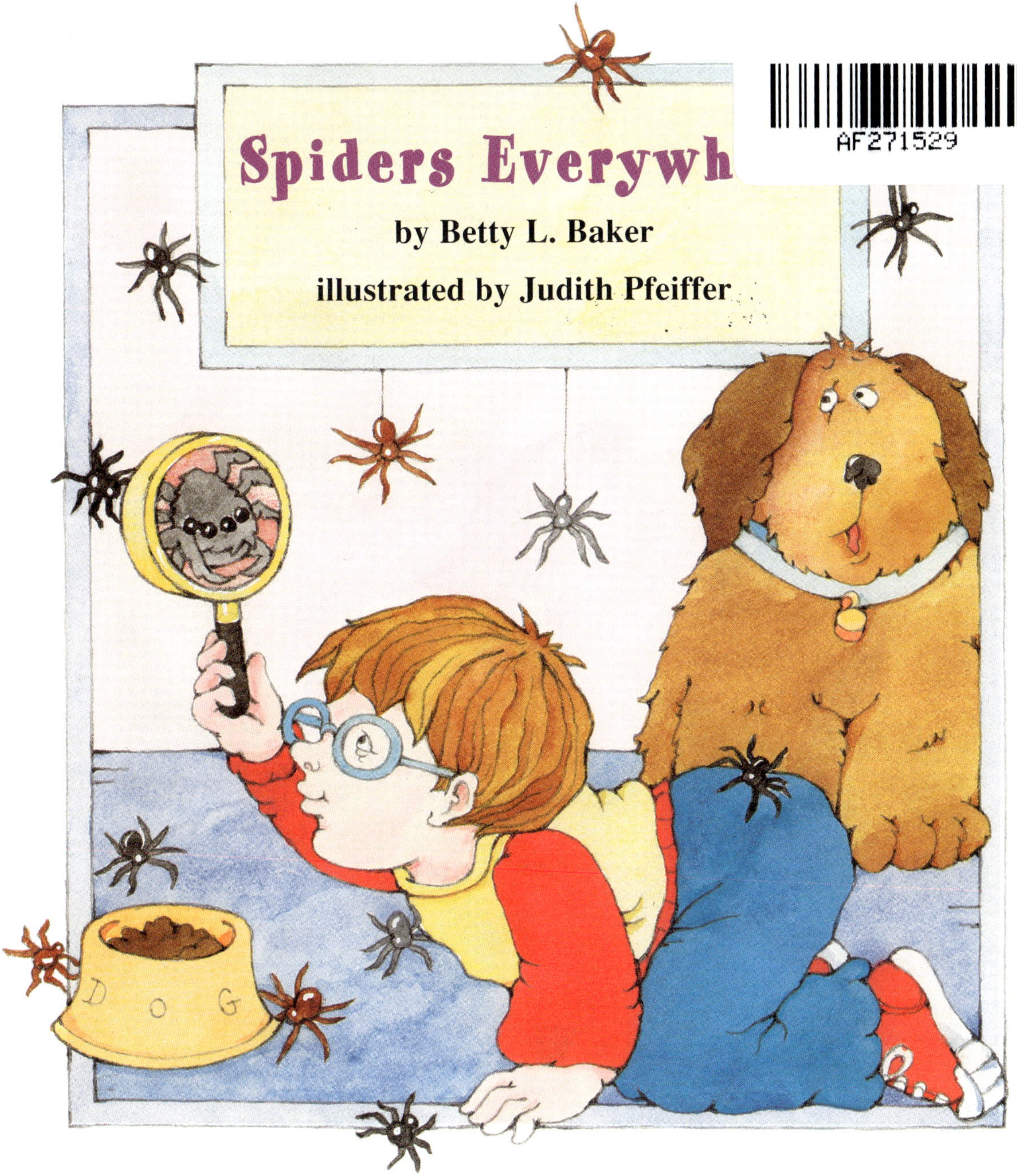

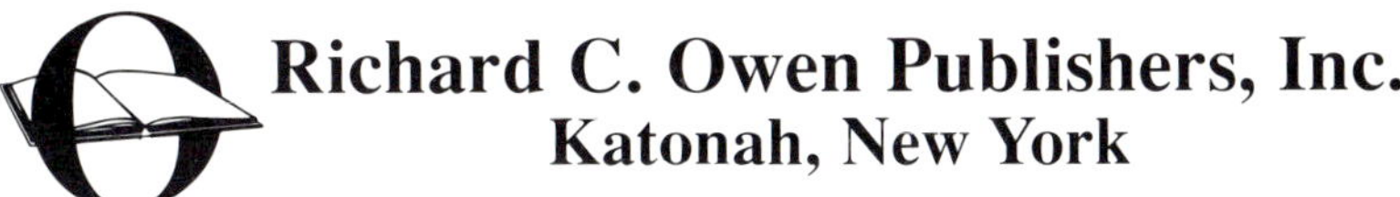

Richard C. Owen Publishers, Inc.
Katonah, New York

Spiders at the window.

Spiders on the floor.

Spiders spinning spider webs
across the kitchen door.

Spiders creeping.
Spiders crawling.

Spiders climbing.

Spiders falling.
Spiders falling from their web.

Oh my gosh!
They're on my head!